Easy Keto Snacks

The Ultimate Low-Carb Cookbook with Best Collection of Quick Ketogenic Appetizers, Energy Boosting Treats & Fat Bombs to Promote Weight Loss, Fat Burning and Healthy Eating

Kaitlyn Donnelly

Disclaimer

The recipes and information in this book are provided for educational purposes only. Please always consult a licensed professional before making changes to your lifestyle or diet. The author and/or publisher shall have neither liability nor responsibility to anyone with respect to any loss or damage caused or alleged to be caused directly or indirectly by the information contained in this book. All trademarks and brands within this book are for clarifying purposes only and are owned by the owners themselves, not affiliated with this document.

Images from shutterstock.com

CONTENTS

INTRODUCTION

Have you ever wanted to have more energy in your day, feel better, and look better? Many people have found a way to achieve a better life with a simple diet. There is no magic pill; rather, it is as simple as developing an eating plan that gives your body the nutrients it needs.

What is this magic eating plan? It is known as the Ketogenic Diet. While most of us are accustomed to the old food guide pyramids and the newer plate renditions released by health and government institutions, many have become frustrated with a lack of improvement in health despite following these guidelines. If you're looking to lose weight, lower your blood glucose, impact your neurological health, or just feel better overall, the keto diet is sure to help!

Fat bombs are high fat, low carb snacks that you can use as a quick breakfast, a quick mid-afternoon snack, a pre- or post-workout snack, or as extra fuel during your day. Fat bombs can be savory or sweet, but they are always made from healthy fats and low carb ingredients. Savory fat bombs will indulge the senses and anchor blood sugars to a steady low number!

Some of the savory treats are really a small meal in themselves, designed to accommodate the demands of busy lifestyles. Fat bombs double as great appetizers for family and friends, or healthy snacks for kids. Now everyone can relish the benefits of this way of eating and stay away from highly processed and sugary foods.

This book offers over 80 delicious low-carb recipes that will enable you to stay true to a ketogenic way of life. These keto snacks are truly the secret weapon every healthy eater should have in his or her arsenal to eat clean, stay full, and feel absolutely satisfied instead of deprived. It's time to embrace not only a diet but a new and healthy way of life!

CHAPTER 1. General Overview

A Closer Look at the Ketogenic Diet

A ketogenic diet is not only one of the popular diets that you've heard of, but it is also considered one of the easiest diets to stick to and helps boost the way you feel. The diet consists of high fat, medium protein, and low carbohydrates. It is the way to make your body burn fat instead of carbohydrates. This causes it to have more fuel to burn throughout the day, so you're able to have more energy than before. This diet is also one of the best ways to shed the fat and lose the pounds.

The fat in the body is converted into fatty acids that are used within the liver. They are then passed through the body as ketones that can be used as glucose sugar, instead of artificial sugars.
This helps the body grow and repair itself easily. It is also something that provides the body with enough calories to burn throughout the day without having excess calories.

One of the most important things that you have to understand about this diet is how ketosis works. Ketosis is the essence of the diet.

When the body is in a ketotic state, it means that the body is going to break down the body's stored fat in order to provide it with the energy that it needs. It also means that the body is providing itself with a way to use the fats that you eat in your food source, instead of the carbohydrates that are normally found in the food. What exactly is the ketogenic diet?

Originally developed in the early 1920s to treat epileptic seizures, the diet fell out of favor in the medical establishment once antiseizure medications became available. More than seventy years later, it was rediscovered as an effective alternative to pharmaceuticals. Since then, it has grown in popularity and has received increasing media attention for the variety of maladies that it can treat.

Crash Course in Your Macronutrients

As you learn more about keto-friendly foods and get used to ketogenic living, it'll be easier for you to understand what and how much you should be eating. Here's a crash course in what your daily macronutrients—carbs, protein, and fat—should look like.

✓ **Carbohydrates (5% to 10%)**

Each person's carb tolerance is different. Your challenge is to find your "ideal" carb intake. As you begin your keto diet, start with a low level of net carbs to ensure you quickly enter ketosis—the state in which your body produces ketone bodies. A good goal would be about 20 grams of net carbs per day. You can purchase a blood ketone meter (or urine ketone strips, which are less accurate) that will allow you to measure your ketones after about two or three days of sticking to your new low-carb lifestyle. Start adding net carbs (about 5 grams each week) until you can detect only a very low level of ketones or none at all. This is usually the quickest, most reliable way to discover your net carbs limit. You can find blood ketone meters and urine ketone strips via online retailers, such as Amazon.

✓ **Protein (15% to 30%)**

The amount of dietary protein you need can be determined by your body weight and activity level. People who are physically active have higher protein requirements than those with sedentary lifestyles. A more accurate estimate, especially for people with high body fat, can be found by calculating protein intake from lean mass, which is determined as total body weight minus body fat.

Consuming enough protein is good for preserving and building muscle mass, but eating excessive amounts of protein are likely to put you out of ketosis because your body will convert excessive protein into glycogen.

✓ **How Many Grams of Protein per Day?**

If your weight is in pounds, then multiply it by 0.6 to get the minimum amount of protein *in grams* you should eat each day. For the maximum amount, multiply your body weight by 1 (i.e., the same numeral as that of your weight but in grams). If your weight is in kilograms, then just multiply it by 1.3 or 2.2 to get the same range. Although this rule applies to the majority of people, protein requirements for athletes are higher. Make sure you eat at least the minimum amount of protein to prevent loss of muscle tissue during the diet. In general, the more active you are, the closer you should be to eating at your upper limit.

✓ **Fat (60% to 75%)**

Your daily fat intake should make up your remaining energy needs: it acts as "filler" for your energy requirements. Ideal fat intake varies for each individual and depends on your personal goal. In fact, you won't need to count fat intake or calories on a ketogenic diet, as you'll be unlikely to overeat: eating foods naturally low in carbs, moderate in protein, and high in fat will keep you satisfied longer. Studies have shown that protein and fats are the most satiating nutrients, while carbohydrates are the least satiating. Fat provides a supply of energy with no insulin spikes. That's why you won't suffer any cravings or energy and mood swings as you would on a calorie-restricted low-fat diet.

Diet Guidelines

Following are some of the best ways to stay in ketosis and get the most out of your ketogenic experience. These tips will help you survive what's known as "keto flu." During your first few days, or up to a week, of ketosis, you may feel a bit tired, sluggish, and dizzy as your body adjusts to producing and burning ketones as energy instead of carbohydrates.

- **Stick to your macros.** The daily 10/20/70 ratio is worth sticking to because it works. Too many carbs and you won't burn fat. Too much protein and it won't burn off if you don't use it. Not enough fat and you won't be full. All these problems add up to less energy. The recommended ratio allows for a whole food approach to ketosis that includes alkalizing green veggies, which break down the acids in meat.

- **Keep your electrolytes up.** Electrolytes are the minerals in our blood that keep us hydrated and keep our nerves and muscles working properly in balance. By producing ketones, you'll be flushing out more electrolytes than usual. This means you should increase your salt intake while following keto because your body won't retain sodium as it used to. Most keto dieters do this by drinking chicken broth or bouillon daily, especially in the first few weeks of ketosis while the body is adjusting. If you feel achy in the first week on keto while going through carbohydrate withdrawal, bouillon helps. Many keto'ers use magnesium supplements as well.

- **Drink lots of water.** Drinking water is one of those things that everyone tells you to do, and you don't take it seriously until you end up with a kidney stone! I promise that drinking two to three liters of water every day will make your body feel clean, full, and hydrated and keep your bowels moving, as well as help you lose weight faster if that's what you're on keto for.

- **Keep track of what you eat.** Measuring what you eat turns any diet into a game. Use apps to track your meals and measure your macros at the end of the day. There's also an app called Quip, which you can use to make shopping lists. It includes check marks that allow you to reuse your shopping list every week.

- **Eat your calories.** Don't try to do a low-calorie ketogenic diet, or you'll end up without any fuel. Fat is your new fuel. Without it, you'll not only be hungry, but you also won't lose weight. Many people on a keto diet eat 1,800 calories or more per day, and I find that eating less actually makes me stop losing weight. But don't overindulge, either. You won't likely lose weight eating 5,000 calories a day.

- **Stock up on healthy fats.** Fat is a dirty word in our society. But there are plenty of good fats out there. Cook everything in ghee, which is lactose- and casein-free clarified butter, high in anti-inflammatory omega-3 fatty acids. For times when you run out of this magical golden buttery oil, keep a backup of coconut oil and olive oil. Avoid processed oils like vegetable, sunflower seed, soybean, and corn—they are high in inflammatory omega-6s, which in turn destroy the healthy omega-3s in your body.

- **Invest in certified organic, grass-fed, and free-range products.** I'm not trying to go all crunchy granola on you, but now that your diet is exchanging highly refined carbohydrates for mostly fats and proteins, you'll want to pay extra-special attention to the quality of those ingredients. I'll identify such ingredients in most of the recipes, and I recommend you buy them if your budget allows.

- **Stick to real food, not low-carb products.** If you check the label of most low-carb products—unless they're also paleo products—you'll be shocked at their ingredients, such as unpronounceable chemical additives. You can control what goes into your body by making your own meals and sticking to whole foods.

CHAPTER 2. Recipes

Chorizo & Avocado Fat Bombs

Prep time: 15 minutes (+ 30 minutes)

Cooking time: 8 minutes

Servings: 4

Nutrients per serving:

Total Carbs – 9.5 g

Net Carbs – 2.7 g

Fat – 38.9 g

Protein – 11.4 g

Calories – 419

Ingredients:

- 3½ oz Spanish chorizo sausage, diced
- 2 large hard-boiled eggs, diced
- ¼ cup unsalted butter
- 2 tbsp mayonnaise
- 1 tbsp lemon juice
- 2 tbsp chives, chopped
- Salt, cayenne pepper to taste
- 4 avocado halves, pitted

Instructions:

1. In a hot pan, fry the chorizo for 5 minutes. Set aside.
2. In a mixing bowl, combine all ingredients. Season with salt and cayenne pepper. Mash together with a fork. Refrigerate for 30 minutes, and then fill each avocado half with ¼ of the mixture.
3. Serve one-quarter of the mixture on top of each avocado half.

Brie Hazelnut Balls

Prep time: 2 hours 5 minutes

Cooking time: none

Servings: 6

Nutrients per serving:

Total Carbs – 2 g

Net Carbs – 0 g

Fat – 11 g

Protein – 5 g

Calories – 121

Ingredients:

- 4 oz Brie
- 2 oz hazelnuts, toasted
- ⅛ tsp fresh thyme, finely chopped

Instructions:

1. In a food processor, combine all ingredients until a coarse, doughy mixture is formed, about 30 seconds.
2. Scrape mixture and transfer to a bowl, then refrigerate 2 hours.
3. Form into 6 balls.
4. Serve or refrigerate up to 3 days.

Blue Cheese Turkey Dressed Eggs

Prep time: 1 hour 20 minutes

Cooking time: 12 minutes

Servings: 6

Nutrients per serving:

Total Carbs – 3.9 g

Net Carbs – 0.6 g

Fat – 11.5 g

Protein – 14 g

Calories – 167

Ingredients:

- 6 hard-boiled eggs
- 2 green onions
- 6 oz smoked turkey breast, chopped
- ½ cup blue cheese, crumbled
- 2 Tbsp Blue cheese dressing
- ¼ cup mayonnaise
- 2 Tbsp hot mustard
- ½ rib celery

Instructions:

1. Chop smoked turkey breast and the celery.
2. Slice eggs in half lengthwise, scrape the yolks out into a bowl. Add the remaining ingredients except for the green onions.
3. Grate the green onions over the mixture. Mix all ingredients together.
4. With the teaspoon fill egg halves with the mixture.
5. Refrigerate for one hour. Serve.

Nutty Bacon Baskets

Prep time: 15 minutes

Cooking time: 20 minutes

Servings: 6

Nutrients per serving:

Total Carbs – 3 g

Net Carbs – 1.5 g

Fat – 44 g

Protein – 9 g

Calories – 437

Ingredients:

- 12 slices bacon, 6 cut in half
- 4 slices cooked bacon, chopped into bits
- 1 Tbsp butter
- ½ cup pecans
- ½ cup macadamia nuts
- ¼ tsp granulated garlic
- ⅛ tsp freshly ground black pepper

Instructions:

1. Preheat oven to 400°F.
2. In a standard-sized muffin tin, place half-strips bacon in an X shape in the bottom of 6 cups. Line those same cups with 1 full slice bacon along with the inside of the cup vertically.
3. Place a cookie sheet underneath muffin tin and bake cups 15 minutes until slightly browned and crisp.
4. While cups are baking, melt butter over medium-low heat in a medium skillet. Add nuts, garlic, and pepper and cook 4-5 minutes. Remove from heat.
5. Once cooled, coarsely chop nut mixture and combine with bacon bits.
6. Divide nut mixture between cups and serve.

Crab Cakes

Prep time: 40 minutes

Cooking time: 30 minutes

Servings: 4

Nutrition facts per serving:

Total Carbs – 5 g

Net Carbs – 4.6 g

Fat – 10 g

Protein – 19 g

Calories – 203

Ingredients:

- 1 lb crabmeat
- 1 egg
- 1 Tbsp Worcestershire sauce
- 1 Tbsp mayonnaise
- 1 Tbsp parsley
- Salt to taste

Instructions:

1. In a bowl mix together egg, Worcester- shire sauce, mayonnaise, parsley and season with salt.
2. Add in crabmeat, mix and form into cakes.
3. Place onto a baking sheet lined up with parchment paper.
4. Refrigerate for 30 minutes.
5. Bake for 30 minutes or until heated through at 375°F.

Tomato & Olive Fat Bombs

Prep time: 15 minutes (+ 30 minutes)

Cooking time: none

Servings: 6

Nutrients per serving:

Total Carbs – 3 g

Net Carbs – 1.9 g

Fat – 18.1 g

Protein – 4.2 g

Calories – 178

Ingredients:

- 3½ oz full-fat cream cheese
- ¼ cup unsalted butter
- ¼ cup Manchego cheese, grated
- ¼ cup sun-dried tomatoes, drained, chopped
- ¼ cup green olives, pitted, sliced
- 2 tbsp capers, drained
- 1 garlic clove, crushed
- ⅓ cup flaked almonds, raw or toasted
- Pepper to taste

Instructions:

1. In a food processor, blend the cream cheese and butter until smooth.
2. Add the next five ingredients. Season with pepper. Mix well. Refrigerate for 30 minutes.
3. Make 6 balls out of the mixture. Roll each ball in the almond flakes. Serve.

Creamy Olive Balls

Prep time: 40 minutes

Cooking time: none

Servings: 6

Nutrients per serving:

Total Carbs – 6 g

Net Carbs – 2 g

Fat – 4 g

Protein – 3 g

Calories – 71

Ingredients:

- 6 large kalamata olives, pitted
- 2 Tbsp cream cheese
- 1 Tbsp coconut oil, melted
- 2 Tbsp hemp hearts

Instructions:

1. Place olives, cream cheese, and coconut oil in a food processor and pulse until well mixed.
2. Refrigerate mixture for 30 minutes, or until it solidifies.
3. Once the mixture is solid, remove from refrigerator and shape into 6 balls.
4. Place hemp hearts on a medium plate and roll individual balls through to coat.
5. Serve immediately or refrigerate in an airtight container up to 4 days.

Bacon Maple Pancake Balls

Prep time: 10 minutes

Cooking time: none

Servings: 6

Nutrients per serving:

Total Carbs – 1 g

Net Carbs – 0 g

Fat – 13 g

Protein – 6 g

Calories – 148

Ingredients:

- 3 oz bacon, cooked
- 3 oz cream cheese
- ½ tsp maple flavor
- ¼ tsp salt
- 3 Tbsp crushed pecans

Instructions:

1. On a cutting board, chop bacon into small pieces.
2. In a bowl, combine cream cheese and bacon with maple flavor and salt. Mix well with a fork.
3. Form mixture into 6 balls.
4. Place crushed pecans on a medium plate and roll individual balls through to coat evenly.
5. Serve immediately or refrigerate up to 3 days.

Curried Tuna Balls

Prep time: 10 minutes

Cooking time: none

Servings: 6

Nutrients per serving:

Total Carbs – 1 g

Net Carbs – 0 g

Fat – 8 g

Protein – 5 g

Calories – 93

Ingredients:

- 3 oz tuna in oil, drained
- 2 oz cream cheese
- ¼ tsp curry powder, divided
- 1 oz crumbled macadamia nuts

Instructions:

1. In a small food processor, mix tuna, cream cheese, and half the curry powder until smooth, about 30 seconds.
2. Form mixture into 6 balls.
3. Place crumbled macadamia nuts and remaining curry powder on a medium plate and roll individual balls through to coat evenly.
4. Serve or refrigerate up to 3 days.

Bacon Jalapeño Balls

Prep time: 10 minutes

Cooking time: none

Servings: 6

Nutrients per serving:

Total Carbs – 1 g

Net Carbs – 0.5 g

Fat – 11 g

Protein – 7 g

Calories – 135

Ingredients:

- 3 oz bacon, cooked, fat reserved
- 3 oz cream cheese
- 2 Tbsp bacon fat, reserved
- 1 tsp jalapeño pepper, seeded, finely chopped
- 1 Tbsp cilantro, finely chopped

Instructions:

1. On a cutting board, chop bacon into small pieces.
2. In a bowl, combine cream cheese, bacon fat, jalapeño, and cilantro. Mix well with a fork.
3. Form mixture into 6 balls.
4. Place bacon pieces on a medium plate and roll individual balls through to coat evenly.
5. Serve immediately or refrigerate up to 3 days.

Egg Tapenade Balls

Prep time: 40 minutes

Cooking time: none

Servings: 6

Nutrients per serving:

Total Carbs – 5 g

Net Carbs – 2 g

Fat – 6 g

Protein – 5 g

Calories – 86

Ingredients:

- 2 large eggs
- 12 large kalamata olives, pitted
- 3 oz anchovy fillet
- 1 Tbsp coconut oil, melted
- 1 Tbsp chia seeds

Instructions:

1. Place eggs, olives, anchovy fillet, and coconut oil in a food processor and pulse until mixed but not over blended.
2. Refrigerate mixture for 30 minutes, or until it solidifies.
3. Once the egg mixture is solid, remove from refrigerator and shape into 6 balls.
4. Place chia seeds on a medium plate and roll individual balls through to coat.
5. Serve immediately or refrigerate in an airtight container up to 4 days.

Avocado, Macadamia, & Prosciutto Balls

Prep time: 7 minutes

Cooking time: none

Servings: 6

Nutrients per serving:

Total Carbs – 5 g

Net Carbs – 2 g

Fat – 17 g

Protein – 3 g

Calories – 170

Ingredients:

- 4 oz macadamia nuts
- 4 oz avocado pulp
- 1 oz cooked prosciutto, crumbled
- ¼ tsp freshly ground black pepper

Instructions:

1. In a small food processor, pulse macadamia nuts until evenly crumbled. Divide in half.
2. In a small bowl, combine avocado, half the macadamia nuts, prosciutto crumbles, and pepper. Mix well with a fork.
3. Form mixture into 6 balls.
4. Place remaining crumbled macadamia nuts on a medium plate and roll individual balls through to coat evenly.
5. Serve immediately.

For the Love of Pork Bombs

Prep time: 1 hour 15 minutes

Cooking time: 10 minutes

Servings: 12

Nutrients per serving:

Total Carbs – 2 g

Net Carbs – 1 g

Fat – 18 g

Protein – 6 g

Calories – 192

Ingredients:

- 8 slices bacon
- 8 oz Braunschweiger, at room temperature
- ¼ cup pistachio, chopped
- 6 oz cream cheese, at room temperature
- 1 tsp Dijon mustard

Instructions:

1. In a skillet, cook the bacon for 5 minutes per side. Drain on paper towels and let cool. Once cooled, crumble bacon.
2. Place Braunschweiger with pistachios in a small food processor and pulse until just combined.
3. In a small mixing bowl, use a hand blender to whip cream cheese and Dijon mustard until fluffy.
4. Divide meat mixture into 12 equal servings. Roll into balls and cover in a thin layer of cream cheese mixture.
5. Chill at least 1 hour. When ready to serve, place bacon bits on a medium plate, roll balls through to coat evenly, and enjoy.
6. Fat bombs can be refrigerated in an airtight container up to 4 days.

Crispy Bacon Fat Bombs

Prep time: 10 minutes (+30 minutes)

Cooking time: 3 minutes

Servings: 4

Nutrients per serving:

Total Carbs – 1.4 g

Net Carbs – 0.5 g

Fat – 12.9 g

Protein – 5.7 g

Calories – 141

Ingredients:

- 4 thick bacon slices
- 4 oz cream cheese
- 1 green chile, seeded, chopped
- 1 tsp onion powder
- Salt and pepper to taste

Instructions:

1. Cook the bacon in a skillet for 3 minutes. Let cool, then crumble. Reserve the bacon fat.
2. In a bowl, combine the remaining ingredients. Add the bacon fat and mix.
3. Shape the mixture into 4 fat bombs. Refrigerate for 30 min.
4. Roll the fat bombs in the crumbled bacon. Serve.

Pizza Balls

Prep time: 8 minutes

Cooking time: none

Servings: 6

Nutrients per serving:

Total Carbs – 1 g

Net Carbs – 0 g

Fat – 8 g

Protein – 3 g

Calories – 82

Ingredients:

- 2 oz fresh mozzarella
- 2 oz cream cheese
- 1 Tbsp olive oil
- 1 tsp tomato paste
- 6 large kalamata olives, pitted
- 12 fresh basil leaves

Instructions:

1. In a food processor, mix all ingredients except basil until they form a smooth cream, about 30 seconds.
2. Form mixture into 6 balls.
3. Place 1 basil leaf on top and bottom of each ball and secure with a toothpick.
4. Serve or refrigerate up to 3 days.

Bacon Ranch Fat Bombs

Prep time: 15 minutes (+ 2 hours)

Cooking time: 15 minutes

Servings: 4

Nutrients per serving:

Total Carbs – 9.5 g

Net Carbs – 2.7 g

Fat – 38.9 g

Protein – 11.4 g

Calories – 419

Ingredients:

- 8 oz full-fat cream cheese, softened
- 1 tbsp ranch dressing dry mix
- 2 slices bacon

Instructions:

1. Preheat the oven to 375°F.
2. Cook the bacon strips on a baking tray for 15 minutes. Let cool, then crumble.
3. In a bowl, add cream cheese and sprinkle with ranch dressing dry mix. Stir in the bacon. Mix thoroughly.
4. Form a ball out of 1 tbsp of the mixture. Repeat to form 3 more bombs. Refrigerate for 2 hours. Serve.

Salmon Mascarpone Balls

Prep time: 7 minutes

Cooking time: none

Servings: 6

Nutrients per serving:

Total Carbs – 1 g

Net Carbs – 0 g

Fat – 5 g

Protein – 3 g

Calories – 65

Ingredients:

- 3 oz smoked salmon, chopped
- 3 oz mascarpone
- ½ tsp maple flavor
- ½ tsp chives, chopped
- 3 Tbsp hemp hearts

Instructions:

1. In a small food processor, combine salmon, mascarpone, maple flavor, and chives. Pulse a few times until blended together.
2. Form mixture into 6 balls.
3. Put hemp hearts on a medium plate and roll individual balls through to coat evenly.
4. Serve immediately or refrigerate up to 3 days.

Bacon, Artichoke & Onion Fat Bombs

Prep time: 15 minutes (+ 30 minutes)

Cooking time: 8 minutes

Servings: 4

Nutrients per serving:

Total Carbs – 10 g

Net Carbs – 4 g

Fat – 39.6 g

Protein – 6.6 g

Calories – 408

Ingredients:

- 2 bacon slices
- 2 tbsp ghee
- ½ large onion, peeled, diced
- 1 garlic clove, minced
- ⅓ cup canned artichoke hearts, sliced
- ¼ cup sour cream
- ¼ cup mayonnaise
- 1 tbsp lemon juice
- ¼ cup Swiss cheese, grated
- Salt, pepper to taste
- 4 avocado halves, pitted

Instructions:

1. In a hot skillet, fry the bacon for 5 minutes. Let cool, then crumble.
2. Cook the onion and garlic using ghee for 3 minutes.
3. Combine the onion and garlic with the bacon and the remaining ingredients. Mix well. Season with salt and pepper. Refrigerate 30 minutes. Fill the avocado halves with the mixture and serve.

Spicy Bacon and Avocado Balls

Prep time: 45 minutes

Cooking time: 8 minutes

Servings: 6

Nutrients per serving:

Total Carbs – 3 g

Net Carbs – 1 g

Fat – 18 g

Protein – 3 g

Calories – 181

Ingredients:

- 4 slices bacon
- 1 medium avocado
- 2 Tbsp coconut oil
- 1 Tbsp bacon fat
- 1 Tbsp green onions, finely chopped
- 2 Tbsp cilantro, finely chopped
- 1 small jalapeño pepper, seeded, finely chopped
- ¼ tsp sea salt

Instructions:

1. Over medium heat, cook bacon until golden, about 4 minutes each side.
2. Drain bacon on a paper towel. Save bacon fat for later.
3. Once bacon is cool, chop 2 slices into crumbles.

4. Cut remaining 2 slices into 3 pieces each.
5. Smash avocado with a fork in a small bowl.
6. Add coconut oil and cooled bacon fat to avocado.
7. Add onion, cilantro, jalapeño, salt, and bacon crumbles. Blend well.
8. Refrigerate for 30 minutes.
9. Form mixture into 6 balls.
10. Place remaining 6 bacon pieces on a plate, then top each with an avocado ball.
11. Serve or refrigerate up to 3 days.

Brie Cheese Fat Bombs

Prep time: 15 minutes (+ 30 minutes)

Cooking time: 3 minutes

Servings: 6

Nutrients per serving:

Total Carbs – 1.7 g

Net Carbs –1.4 g

Fat – 16.2 g

Protein – 3.3 g

Calories – 158

Ingredients:

- 2 oz full-fat cream cheese
- ¼ cup unsalted butter
- ½ cup Brie cheese, chopped
- 1 tbsp ghee
- 1 white onion, diced
- 1 garlic clove, minced
- ½ tsp paprika
- Salt, pepper to taste
- 6 lettuce leaves

Instructions:

1. In a food processor, mix the cream cheese and butter. Transfer to a bowl. Mix in the Brie.
2. In a pan, add onion and garlic and cook 3 minutes over medium heat with ghee. Let cool. Once cooled, combine with the cheese and butter mixture.
3. Season with the spices and mix. Refrigerate 30 minutes.
4. Make 6 fat bombs out of the mixture. Serve on lettuce leaves.

Salted Caramel and Brie Balls

Prep time: 5 minutes

Cooking time: 5 minutes

Servings: 6

Nutrients per serving:

Total Carbs – 1 g

Net Carbs – 0 g

Fat – 12 g

Protein – 5 g

Calories – 130

Ingredients:

- 4 oz Brie, roughly chopped
- 2 oz salted macadamia nuts
- ½ tsp caramel flavor
- 1 Tbsp butter
- 1 large apple, chopped

Instructions:

1. In a food processor, mix all ingredients until a coarse mix forms, about 30 seconds.
2. Form mixture into 6 balls.
3. In a saucepan, melt the butter, then add the chopped apples. Cook until apples for about 5 minutes.
4. Spoon the apples over the brie balls. Serve or refrigerate up to 3 days.

Easy Savory Fat Bombs

Prep time: 20 minutes (+ 1 hour)

Cooking time: 30 minutes

Servings: 6

Nutrients per serving:

Total Carbs – 0.9 g

Net Carbs – 0.8 g

Fat – 14.6 g

Protein – 2.7 g

Calories – 136

Ingredients:

- 3½ oz full-fat cream cheese
- ¼ cup unsalted butter
- 2 bacon slices
- 1 garlic clove, crushed
- 1 spring onion, sliced
- Salt, pepper to taste
- 6 lettuce leaves

Instructions:

1. In a food processor, mix the cream cheese and butter. Transfer to a bowl.
2. Preheat the oven to 325°F.
3. Cook the bacon slices on a baking sheet for 30 minutes. Reserve the grease and crumble the bacon in a bowl.
4. Add the garlic, sliced onion, bacon (reserve some for later), and bacon grease from the sheet to the bowl with the butter mixture. Season with salt and pepper. Mix well. Refrigerate for 1 hour.
5. Make 6 fat bombs out of the mixture. Roll them in reserved crumbled bacon. Serve.

Carbonara Balls

Prep time: 8 minutes

Cooking time: none

Servings: 6

Nutrients per serving:

Total Carbs – 1 g

Net Carbs – 0 g

Fat – 12 g

Protein – 8 g

Calories – 148

Ingredients:

- 3 oz bacon, cooked
- 3 oz mascarpone
- 2 large hard-boiled egg yolks
- ¼ tsp freshly ground black pepper

Instructions:

1. On a cutting board, chop bacon into small pieces.
2. In a small bowl, combine mascarpone, egg yolks, and pepper. Mix well with a fork.
3. Form mascarpone mixture into 6 balls.
4. Place bacon crumbles on a medium plate and roll individual balls through to coat evenly.
5. Serve immediately or refrigerate up to 3 days.

Stilton & Chive Fat Bombs

Prep time: 15 minutes (+ 30 minutes)

Cooking time: none

Servings: 6

Nutrients per serving:

Total Carbs – 1.1 g

Net Carbs – 0.8 g

Fat – 16.2 g

Protein – 5 g

Calories – 157

Ingredients:

- 3½ oz full-fat cream cheese
- ¼ cup unsalted butter
- ½ cup Stilton, crumbled
- 2 spring onions, chopped
- 1 tbsp parsley, chopped
- ⅓ cup fresh chives, chopped

Instructions:

1. In a food processor, mix the cream cheese and butter.
2. Add the crumbled blue cheese, spring onions, and parsley. Mix well. Refrigerate for 30 minutes.
3. Make 6 balls out of the mixture. Roll each ball in the chives. Serve.

Baked Creamy Shrimps with Artichoke Hearts

Prep time: 5 minutes

Cooking time: 40 minutes

Servings: 16

Nutrients per serving:

Total Carbs – 6.3 g

Net Carbs – 1.6 g

Fat – 11 g

Protein – 8 g

Calories – 150

Ingredients:

- 6 oz shrimp, precooked
- 2 Tbsp butter
- 1 can artichoke hearts, chopped
- 6 scallions
- ½ cup mayonnaise
- ½ cup sour cream
- 1 cup Cheddar cheese, shredded
- 1¼ cup Parmesan cheese, shredded
- 1 Tbsp garlic, minced
- 1 tsp red pepper flakes
- 1 tsp garlic powder

Instructions:

1. Preheat oven to 350°F.
2. In a frying pan, sauté shrimp over medium heat with butter and red pepper flakes for 5-10 minutes.
3. Chop the artichoke hearts.
4. In a bowl, combine all ingredient and mix well.
5. Pour the mixture in a baking dish and bake for 30 minutes. Serve hot.

Olive Cheese balls

Prep time: 5 minutes

Cooking time: 15 minutes

Servings: 12

Nutrients per serving:

Total Carbs – 5 g

Net Carbs – 4.3 g

Fat – 8 g

Protein – 4 g

Calories – 110

Ingredients:

- 24 pimento stuffed olives
- 1 cup Cheddar, shredded
- 2 Tbsp butter, softened
- ½ cup Keto friendly flour (almond/coconut/etc)
- Cayenne pepper to taste

Instructions:

1. In a medium bowl combine cheese and butter, and stir in the flour. Mix to combine and season with pepper.
2. Wrap the cheese, butter and flour mixture around each olive.
3. Arrange the olive cheese balls on a baking sheet lined with parchment paper.
4. Bake for 15 minutes at 400°F.

Sunbutter Balls

Prep time: 20 minutes

Cooking time: none

Servings: 12

Nutrients per serving:

Total Carbs – 2 g

Net Carbs – 1 g

Fat – 13

Protein – 2 g

Calories – 124

Ingredients:

- 6 Tbsp mascarpone
- 3 Tbsp sunflower seed butter
- 6 Tbsp coconut oil, softened
- 3 Tbsp unsweetened shredded coconut flakes

Instructions:

1. In a medium bowl, mix mascarpone, sunflower seed butter, and coconut oil until smooth paste forms.
2. Shape paste into walnut-sized balls.
3. Spread coconut flakes on a medium plate and roll individual balls through to coat evenly.

Ham & Cheese Fat Bombs

Prep time: 15 minutes (+ 30 minutes)

Cooking time: none

Servings: 6

Nutrients per serving:

Total Carbs – 0.9 g

Net Carbs – 0.7 g

Fat – 16.7 g

Protein – 6.4 g

Calories – 167

Ingredients:

- 3½ oz full-fat cream cheese
- ¼ cup unsalted butter
- ¼ cup Cheddar cheese, grated
- 2 tbsp fresh basil, chopped
- 6 slices Parma ham
- 6 large green olives, pitted
- Pepper to taste

Instructions:

1. In a food processor, blend the cream cheese and butter.
2. Add the Cheddar cheese and basil, mix well. Season with pepper. Refrigerate for 30 minutes.
3. Make 6 balls out of the mixture. Roll each ball with 1 slice of Parma ham, top with 1 olive, piercing it with a toothpick. Serve.

Boiled Eggs and Pancetta Fat Bombs

Prep time: 20 minutes

Cooking time: 15 minutes

Servings: 4

Nutrients per serving:

Total Carbs – 2.2 g

Net Carbs – 0.5 g

Fat – 22 g

Protein – 7.5 g

Calories – 238

Ingredients:

- 4 large slices Pancetta
- 2 hard- boiled free-range eggs
- 1 cup ghee, softened
- 2 Tbsp mayonnaise
- Salt, freshly ground black pepper, to taste
- coconut oil for frying

Instructions:

1. Fry pancetta, 1-2 minutes per side. Remove from the fire and set aside.
2. In a deep bowl, combine ghee and eggs. Mash well with a fork. Add salt, pepper, and mayonnaise. Mix well. Refrigerate for one hour.
3. Make 4 equal balls.
4. Crumble the Pancetta into small pieces. Roll each ball in the Pancetta crumbles.
5. Refrigerate for 30 minutes more. Serve cold.

Veggie & Cheese Fat Bombs

Prep time: 15 minutes (+ 30 minutes)

Cooking time: 6 minutes

Servings: 6

Nutrients per serving:

Total Carbs – 3.6 g

Net Carbs – 3 g

Fat – 16.7 g

Protein – 3.4 g

Calories – 166

Ingredients:

- 3½ oz full-fat cream cheese,
- ¼ cup unsalted butter
- 1 tbsp ghee
- ½ onion, peeled, chopped
- 1 garlic clove, peeled and finely chopped
- ½ cup dried porcini mushrooms
- 2 cups spinach
- Salt, pepper to taste
- ¼ cup hard goat cheese, grated

Instructions:

1. Mix the cream cheese and butter in a food processor.
2. In a pan, cook the onion and garlic with ghee over medium heat for 3 minutes. Add the dried chopped mushrooms and spinach; cook for another 3 min. Set aside to cool.
3. Mix the cream cheese and butter with the cooled mushroom and spinach mixture. Season with salt and pepper. Refrigerate for 30 minutes.
1. Make 5 balls out of the mixture. Roll each ball in the goat cheese. Serve.

Olives and Sun-dried Tomatoes Fat Bombs

Prep time: 2 hours 20 minutes

Cooking time: none

Servings: 4

Nutrients per serving:

Total Carbs – 4 g

Net Carbs – 1 g

Fat – 14 g

Protein – 4.6 g

Calories – 157

Ingredients:

- 1 cup cream cheese
- 1 cup ghee
- 5 Tbsp Parmesan cheese, grated
- ¼ cup sun-dried tomatoes, chopped
- ¼ cup Kalamata olives, pitted
- 3 cloves garlic, crushed
- 3 Tbsp herbs mix (basil, parsley, thyme, oregano, parsnip, mint)
- Salt, freshly ground black pepper, to taste

Instructions:

1. In a bowl, mix the cream cheese and ghee. Set aside for 30-45 minutes to soften. Then mix to combine.
2. Add the chopped Kalamata olives and sun-dried tomatoes.
3. Add in herbs and crushed garlic; season with salt and pepper to taste. Mix well with and place the bowl in the fridge for at least 1 hour.
4. Take the cheese mixture out from the fridge and create 4 balls. Roll each ball in the Parmesan cheese.
5. Refrigerate for 30 minutes. Serve and enjoy.

Barbecue Balls

Prep time: 2 hours 5 minutes

Cooking time: none

Servings: 6

Nutrients per serving:

Total Carbs – 1 g

Net Carbs – 0 g

Fat – 13 g

Protein – 3 g

Calories – 154

Ingredients:

- 4 oz cream cheese
- 4 Tbsp bacon fat
- ½ tsp smoke flavor
- 2 drops stevia glycerite
- ⅛ tsp apple cider vinegar
- 1 Tbsp sweet smoked chili powder
- 3 Tbsp barbecue sauce

Instructions:

1. In a food processor, combine all ingredients except chili powder until a smooth, creamy mixture forms, about 30 seconds.
2. Transfer mixture to a small bowl, then refrigerate 2 hours.
3. Form into 6 balls.
4. Sprinkle balls with chili powder, rolling around to coat all sides. Pour barbecue sauce over balls.
5. Serve or refrigerate up to 3 days.

Prosciutto and Egg Balls

Prep time: 40 minutes

Cooking time: none

Servings: 6

Nutrients per serving:

Total Carbs – 0 g

Net Carbs – 0 g

Fat – 8 g

Protein – 4 g

Calories – 84

Ingredients:

- 2 medium hard-boiled eggs
- 2 Tbsp mayonnaise
- ⅛ tsp black pepper, freshly ground
- ⅛ tsp sea salt
- 1 Tbsp coconut oil, melted
- 6 slices prosciutto, cooked

Instructions:

1. Place eggs, mayonnaise, pepper, and salt in a small bowl. Mash with a fork to mix and combine while still retaining some texture.
2. Pour melted coconut oil into mixture and blend in well.
3. Refrigerate mixture for 30 minutes, or until it solidifies.
4. Once the egg mixture is solid, remove from refrigerator and shape into 6 balls.
5. Wrap the balls in prosciutto slices.
6. Serve or refrigerate up to 4 days.

Pork Belly Fat Bombs

Prep time: 10 minutes (+ 30 minutes)

Cooking time: none

Servings: 6

Nutrients per serving:

Total Carbs – 0.5 g

Net Carbs – 0.3 g

Fat – 26.4 g

Protein – 3.5 g

Calories – 263

Ingredients:

- 3 bacon slices, cut in half widthwise
- 5⅓ oz pork belly, cooked
- ¼ cup mayonnaise
- 1 tbsp Dijon mustard
- 1 tbsp fresh horseradish, grated
- Salt, pepper to taste
- 6 lettuce leaves, for serving

Instructions:

1. Preheat the oven to 325°F.
2. Cook the bacon slices on a baking sheet for 30 minutes. in the oven. Let cool.
3. Crumble the bacon into a dish and set aside.
4. Shred the pork belly into a bowl. Mix in the mayonnaise, mustard, and horseradish. Season with salt and pepper.
5. Divide the mixture into 6 mounds. Top with the crumbled bacon and serve on top of lettuce leaves.

Ham, Sausage, and Cashews Truffles

Prep time: 1 hour 15 minutes

Cooking time: none

Servings: 12

Nutrients per serving:

Total Carbs – 1.5 g

Net Carbs – 0.5 g

Fat – 11 g

Protein – 7 g

Calories – 125

Ingredients:

- 8 slices smoked ham, finely chopped
- 8 oz sausages
- 6 oz cream cheese, softened
- 1 cup cashews, chopped
- 1 tsp Dijon mustard

Instructions:

1. In a food processor, blend sausages and cashews.
2. In a separate bowl, beat the cream cheese and mustard until soft.
3. Roll the sausage mixture into 12 small balls. Take each ball and form layer of cream cheese with your fingers.
4. Refrigerate for about 45-60 minutes.
5. Roll each ball in the finely chopped smoked ham and place on a serving dish. Serve.

Herbed Cheese Fat Bombs

Prep time: 10 minutes (+ 30 minutes)

Cooking time: none

Servings: 5

Nutrients per serving:

Total Carbs – 2 g

Net Carbs – 1.7 g

Fat – 17.1 g

Protein – 3.7 g

Calories – 164

Ingredients:

- 3½ oz full-fat cream cheese
- ¼ cup unsalted butter
- 4 pieces sun-dried tomatoes, drained, chopped
- 4 pitted green olives, chopped
- 2 tsp dried herbs
- 2 garlic cloves, crushed
- 5 tbsp Parmesan cheese, grated
- Salt, pepper to taste

Instructions:

1. Blend together the cream cheese and butter. Transfer to a bowl.
2. Add the next four ingredients. Season with salt and pepper, and mix. Refrigerate for 30 minutes.
3. Make 5 balls out of the mixture. Roll each ball in the Parmesan cheese. Serve.

Cheesy Pesto Fat Bombs

Prep time: 5 minutes (+ 2 hours)

Cooking time: none

Servings: 6

Nutrients per serving:

Total Carbs – 1.6 g

Net Carbs – 1.3 g

Fat – 12.9 g

Protein – 4.3 g

Calories – 123

Ingredients:

- 1 cup full-fat cream cheese
- 2 tbsp basil pesto
- ½ cup Parmesan cheese, grated
- 10 green olives, sliced
- 6 cucumber slices

Instructions:

1. Using a spatula, mix all the ingredients in a bowl until well combined.
2. Serve as a dip with sliced cucumber or other fresh vegetables.
3. You can also refrigerate for 30 minutes, then create balls and roll in Parmesan cheese.
4. Serve as a dip with cucumber slices.

Sour Bacon Fat Bomb Dip

Prep time: 5 minutes

Cooking time: 30 minutes

Servings: 18

Nutrients per serving:

Total Carbs – 1.7 g

Net Carbs – 1.4 g

Fat – 19 g

Protein – 5.5 g

Calories – 197

Ingredients:

- 6 slices bacon, cooked, crumbled
- 2 cups sour cream
- 1 cup cream cheese
- 1½ cups Cheddar cheese, shredded
- 1 cup sliced scallions

Instructions:

1. Preheat oven to 400°F.
2. In a deep bowl, combine all ingredients. Transfer mixture into a baking dish and bake until cheese is bubbling about 25-30 minutes.
3. Once ready, let cool and serve hot.

Savory Salmon Fat Bombs

Prep time: 10 minutes (+ 2 hours)

Cooking time: none

Servings: 6

Nutrients per serving:

Total Carbs – 0.8 g

Net Carbs – 0.7 g

Fat – 15.7 g

Protein – 3.2 g

Calories – 147

Ingredients:

- ½ cup full-fat cream cheese
- ⅓ cup butter, grass-fed
- ½ package (2 oz) smoked salmon
- 1 tbsp fresh lemon juice
- 1-2 tbsp dill, chopped
- 5 lettuce leaves

Instructions:

1. Pulse all ingredients together in a food processor.
2. Line a tray with parchment paper and make fat bombs using about 2½ tbsp of the mixture for each. Refrigerate for 2 hours, garnish with more dill and place on top of lettuce leaves.
3. Serve or store in an airtight container in the fridge for up to a week.

Turkey Bacon and Avocado Stuffed Eggs

Prep time: 1 hour 15 minutes

Cooking time: 12 minutes

Servings: 6

Nutrients per serving:

Total Carbs – 4.4 g

Net Carbs – 0.5 g

Fat – 13 g

Protein – 9 g

Calories – 162

Ingredients:

- 6 hard-boiled eggs
- 1 avocado
- 6 slices smoked turkey bacon
- 2 Tbsp mustard
- 1 Tbsp garlic, minced
- 1 Tbsp lime juice
- 1 Tbsp dried onion flakes
- Cayenne pepper, to taste
- 1 tsp garlic salt

Instructions:

1. In a mixing bowl, mash the avocado.
2. Scrape the yolks out of the eggs and into the mixing bowl. Add in the bacon, mustard, cayenne pepper, lime juice, onion flakes, garlic and garlic salt. Mix well until smooth and creamy.
3. Fill each egg half with the avocado mixture. Refrigerate stuffed eggs for 1 hour. Serve.

Savory Salmon Bites

Prep time: 5 minutes (+ 2 hours)

Cooking time: none

Servings: 12

Nutrients per serving:

Total Carbs – 1 g

Net Carbs – 1 g

Fat – 13 g

Protein – 3 g

Calories – 117

Ingredients:

- 2 oz smoked salmon trimmings.
- 1 cup mascarpone cheese
- ⅔ cup grass-fed butter, softened
- 1 tbsp apple cider vinegar
- 1 tbsp chopped parsley
- Salt to taste

Instructions:

1. Smash the cheese with a fork to soften and add the remaining ingredients.
2. Form into small balls, and place on a tray lined with parchment paper.
3. Put in the fridge for 2 hours. Serve.

Viva Mexico Angels Eggs

Prep time: 1 hour 20 minutes

Cooking time: 12 minutes

Servings: 6

Nutrients per serving:

Total Carbs – 4.5 g

Net Carbs – 0.2 g

Fat – 13.5 g

Protein – 7 g

Calories – 163

Ingredients:

- ¼ cup cream cheese, softened
- 6 slices Pancetta
- 6 large hard-boiled eggs
- 6 Tbsp mayonnaise
- 16 sliced pickled Guajillo chili peppers
- ¼ tsp smoked paprika

Instructions:

1. Chop 4 of the Guajillo chilis and set aside.
2. Remove yolks from hard-boiled eggs and mash them in a medium bowl.
3. Add pancetta, mayonnaise, cream cheese, and chopped Guajillo chili to the bowl. Mix until all ingredients are well incorporated.
4. Fill the egg halves with the mixter and top each egg with a Guajillo chili slice.
5. Sprinkle with paprika and refrigerate for 1 hour. Serve.

Avocado & Egg Fat Bombs

Prep time: 20 minutes (+ 1 hour)

Cooking time: none

Servings: 2

Nutrients per serving:

Total Carbs – 2.5 g

Net Carbs – 1.1 g

Fat –14.8 g

Protein – 2.2 g

Calories – 147

Ingredients:

- 3 large cooked egg yolks
- ½ avocado, peeled, pitted and chopped
- ¼ cup mayonnaise
- 1 tbsp lemon juice
- 2 tbsp spring onions, chopped
- Salt, pepper to taste

Instructions:

1. Boil the eggs for 10 minutes.
2. Halve the eggs. Scoop the egg yolks into a bowl.
3. Blend chopped avocado and the remaining ingredients in a food processor.
4. Mix the avocado mixture with the egg yolks.
5. Enjoy with cucumber slices and chopped spring onion on top, or fill up the egg white halves and make deviled eggs. Serve.

Hot Hot Fat Bombs

Prep time: 20 minutes

Cooking time: 5 minutes

Servings: 6

Nutrients per serving:

Total Carbs – 1.3 g

Net Carbs – 0.6 g

Fat – 16 g

Protein – 4 g

Calories – 165

Ingredients:

- ½ cup Cream cheese
- 4 slices Pepperoni Sausages
- 3 slices smoked bacon
- 1 medium chili pepper
- ½ tsp dried basil
- ¼ tsp onion powder
- ¼ tsp garlic powder
- Salt, pepper, to taste

Instructions:

1. In a frying pan, brown bacon and Peperoni sausages until crisp.
2. Remove bacon and Pepperoni from the pan on a paper lined plate to cool. Keep the remaining grease for later use.
3. Dice chili pepper into small pieces.
4. Combine cream cheese, chilli pepper, and spices. Add the bacon fat in and mix together until a solid mixture is formed. Season with salt and pepper to taste.
5. Crumble bacon and Pepperone slices and set on a plate. Roll cream cheese mixture into 6 balls, then roll the ball into the bacon or Pepperone.

Cheesy Jalapeño Fat Bombs

Prep time: 20 minutes (+ 1 hour)

Cooking time: 30 minutes

Servings: 6

Nutrients per serving:

Total Carbs – 0.9 g

Net Carbs – 0.7 g

Fat – 15 g

Protein – 3.5 g

Calories – 142

Ingredients:

- 3½ oz full-fat cream cheese
- ¼ cup unsalted butter
- 4 bacon slices
- ¼ cup Cheddar cheese, grated
- 2 jalapeño peppers, seeded, chopped

Instructions:

1. Preheat the oven to 325°F. Line a baking sheet with parchment paper.
2. Lay the bacon slices on the parchment. Cook for 30 minutes. in the oven. Crumble the bacon into a bowl. Reserve the grease.
3. Blend together the cream cheese and butter. Transfer to a bowl.
4. Add the Cheddar cheese, jalapeños, and bacon grease. Mix well. Refrigerate for 1 hour.
5. Make 6 fat bombs out of the mixture. Roll them in the bacon crumbs. Refrigerate for 1 hour. Serve.

Wrapped Bacon Rolls

Prep time: 10 minutes

Cooking time: none

Servings: 12

Nutrients per serving:

Total Carbs – 2.7 g

Net Carbs – 0.7 g

Fat – 17.7 g

Protein – 1.78 g

Calories – 174

Ingredients:

- 4 bacon slices
- 6 toasted pecan halves, chopped
- ½ cup unsalted butter
- ½ cup mayonnaise
- Granulated garlic, to taste

Instructions:

1. Divide each bacon slice into 3 equal parts.
2. Spread each bacon slice with unsalted butter. Press pecan pieces into butter.
3. Top with each with mayonnaise, sprinkle with granulated garlic and wrap in rolls. Serve.

Keto Sausage Balls

Prep time: 10 minutes

Cooking time: 20 minutes

Servings: 20

Nutrients per serving:

Total Carbs – 1 g

Net Carbs – 0.2 g

Fat – 11 g

Protein – 6 g

Calories – 124

Ingredients:

- 1 lb breakfast sausage,
- 1 egg
- 1 cup almond flour
- 8 oz Cheddar cheese, grated
- ¼ cup Parmesan, grated
- 1 tbsp butter
- 2 tsp baking powder

Instructions:

1. Preheat oven to 350°F
2. Mix all ingredients in a large bowl.
3. Make 20 sausage balls out of the mixture. Put sausage balls on a baking sheet.
4. Bake for 20 minutes. Serve.

Pancetta Wrapped Provolone Sticks

Prep time: 10 minutes

Cooking time: 3 minutes

Servings: 10

Nutrients per serving:

Total Carbs – 0.4 g

Net Carbs – 0.1 g

Fat – 22 g

Protein – 5.6 g

Calories – 216

Ingredients:

- 4 slices Pancetta bacon
- 2 Frigo string Provolone cheese (or Mozzarela, Kasseri, Emmenthal)
- ½ cup coconut oil for frying

Instructions:

1. Preheat coconut oil to 350°F in a deep fryer.
2. Wrap Provolone around Pancetta and secure with a toothpick.
3. Drop the bacon wrapped cheese in the hot oil and cook about 2-3 minutes, depending on the thickness of your bacon.
4. Remove to a paper towel to cool for a few minutes. Remove the toothpick and serve.

Keto Scotch Eggs

Prep time: 15 minutes

Cooking time: 20 minutes

Servings: 6

Nutrients per serving:

Total Carbs – 0.5 g

Net Carbs – 0.2 g

Fat – 22.5 g

Protein – 28.2 g

Calories – 319

Ingredients:

- 6 eggs, boiled
- 1 lb 2 oz pork, ground
- 2 tsp herbs of choice
- 1 tsp onion flakes
- Salt and pepper to taste

Instructions:

1. Hard-boil the eggs and remove the shells
2. Combine the ground meat, the herbs, spices, and salt and pepper.
3. Coat each egg with enough meat mixture to cover.
4. Sprinkle Scotch eggs with oil in a lined baking tray.
5. Bake at 350°F for 20 minutes. or until golden on all sides. Cool and serve.

Savory Coco Bacon Fat Bombs

Prep time: 40 minutes

Cooking time: none

Servings: 24

Nutrients per serving:

Total Carbs – 0.5 g

Net Carbs – 0.3 g

Fat – 15.9 g

Protein – 0 g

Calories – 261

Ingredients:

- 8 strips cooked crispy bacon, crumbled, divided
- 1 cup cream cheese, softened
- ½ cup butter
- 4 tsp bacon fat
- 4 Tbsp coconut oil
- ¼ cup Splenda

Instructions:

1. In a microwave-safe dish, combine all ingredients and melt slowly in the microwave until smooth. Set aside 1 bacon strip.
2. Pour into a dish or pan and freeze until firm, about 30 minutes.
3. Before serving, remove from freezer, sprinkle with crumbled bacon, slice and serve.

Keto Cheese Meatballs

Prep time: 10 minutes

Cooking time: 10 minutes

Servings: 9

Nutrients per serving:

Total Carbs – 3.6 g

Net Carbs – 2 g

Fat – 28 g

Protein – 46 g

Calories – 444

Ingredients:

- 17 oz beef, ground
- 4 oz mozzarella cheese
- 3 tbsp Parmesan cheese
- 1 tsp garlic powder
- 3 tbsp olive oil
- Salt, pepper to taste

Instructions:

1. Cut the cheese into cubes.
2. Combine the dry ingredients with the ground beef.
3. Roll the cubes of cheese with the beef, making 9 balls.
4. Fry the meatballs in olive oil for 10 minutes. Let chill and serve.

Greek-Style Fat Bomb Balls

Prep time: 20 minutes

Cooking time: none

Servings: 5

Nutrients per serving:

Total Carbs – 2.8 g

Net Carbs – 0.8 g

Fat – 19.8 g

Protein – 3.67 g

Calories – 200

Ingredients:

- 1 cup cream cheese, softened
- 1 cup butter, softened
- 2-3 Tbsp freshly chopped herbs (any combination of basil, thyme, oregano and/or parsley works great) or 2 tsp of dried herbs
- 4 sun-dried tomatoes, drained
- 4 Kalamata olives, pitted, chopped
- 2 cloves garlic, crushed
- Black pepper, to taste
- 1 tsp sea salt
- 5 Tbsp Parmesan cheese, finely grated

Instructions:

1. Mash the butter and cream cheese together with a fork and mix until well combined. Mix in the sun-dried tomatoes and Kalamata olives.
2. Stir in the herbs, garlic, salt, and pepper. Mix and refrigerate for 20-30 minutes.
3. Make 5 balls out from the mixture. A spoon or an ice-cream scooper works well.
4. Place the grated Parmesan cheese in a shallow dish. Roll each ball in the cheese and place on a plate. Serve or store in the fridge in an airtight container for up to a week.

Sesame Fat Bombs

Prep time: 15 minutes (+ 15 minutes)

Cooking time: none

Servings: 4

Nutrients per serving:

Total Carbs – 0.3 g

Net Carbs – 0.2 g

Fat – 4.5 g

Protein – 2 g

Calories – 123

Ingredients:

- 4 oz butter
- 2 tbsp sesame oil
- 1 tsp sea salt
- ¼ tsp chili flakes
- 2 tsp sesame seeds, toasted

Instructions:

1. In a pan, toast sesame seeds 5 minutes. Set aside.
2. In a bowl, mix remaining ingredients. Refrigerate for 15 mins.
3. Make 4 fat bombs out of the mixture. Roll each fat bomb in the toasted sesame seeds. Serve or store in the fridge.

Scrambled Eggs Muffins

Prep time: 45 minutes

Cooking time: none

Servings: 8

Nutrients per serving:

Total Carbs – 0.5 g

Net Carbs – 0.3 g

Fat – 16.9 g

Protein – 7.9 g

Calories – 186

Ingredients:

- 3 strips bacon, cooked, crumbled
- 6 six eggs
- 2 Tbsp coconut oil or butter
- 1 Tbsp butter
- ¼ cup softened cream cheese
- ¼ cup Gouda cheese, shredded

Instructions:

1. In a small bowl, melt the butter and set aside. In a separate bowl, beat the eggs. Add in spices. Melt some butter in a non stick skillet on medium heat and scramble the eggs.
2. Put cooked eggs into another large bowl. Mix in cheeses. Add bacon and stir. Add the melted butter and coconut oil.
3. Pour the batter in mini muffin liners. Place on cookie sheet with or without wax paper, and freeze for about 30 minutes. Serve.

Buttered Bacon Fat Bomb

Prep time: 2 minutes

Cooking time: none

Servings: 1

Nutrients per serving:

Total Carbs –0.7 g

Net Carbs – 0.5 g

Fat – 8.1 g

Protein – 0.8 g

Calories – 77

Ingredients:

- 4 bacon slice
- 4 tbsp Kerrygold butter, unsalted
- 1 tsp garlic powder
- ⅓ cup pecans, toasted, chopped

Instructions:

1. Preheat the oven to 325°F. Cook the bacon slice on a baking sheet for 30 minutes. Crumble the bacon.
2. In a bowl, mix remaining ingredients. Refrigerate for 15 mins.
3. Make 4 fat bombs out of the mixture. Roll each fat bomb in the crumbled bacon. Serve or store in the fridge.

Simple Parmesan Crisps

Prep time: 15 minutes

Cooking time: 15 minutes

Servings: 4

Nutrients per serving:

Total Carbs – 6.4 g

Net Carbs – 0.4 g

Fat – 7.47 g

Protein – 10.4 g

Calories – 135.5

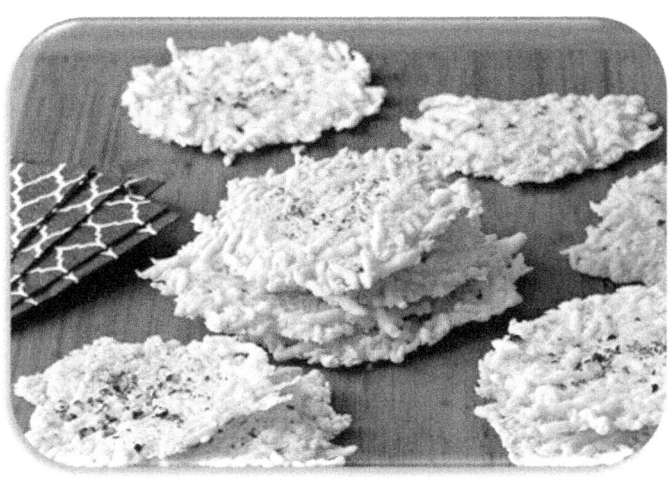

Ingredients:

- 1 cup parmesan cheese
- 4 Tbsp coconut flour
- 1-2 tsp rosemary, oregano, or any herbs of choice, dried or fresh

Instructions:

1. Preheat the oven to 350°F. In a small bowl, combine all ingredients.
2. Scoop one teaspoon at a time of the cheese mixture onto a baking tray lined with parchment paper, leaving a small gap between each. Place in the oven and cook for 10-15 minutes, or until golden brown. Be careful not to burn.
3. Remove from the oven and let cool for 15 minutes. Serve

Salmon & Dill Fat Bombs

Prep time: 5 minutes (+ 30 minutes)

Cooking time: none

Servings: 12

Nutrients per serving:

Total Carbs – 1.4 g

Net Carbs – 0.3 g

Fat – 13.4 g

Protein – 3 g

Calories – 174

Ingredients:

- 1 cup cream cheese
- ⅔ cup butter
- ½ package (2 oz) of smoked salmon
- Lemon juice to taste
- Dill to taste
- Salt to taste

Instructions:

1. Place all ingredients in a food processor and blend.
2. Create small balls with the mixture and put in the refrigerator for 30 minutes. Serve cold.

Smoked Sardine Paté

Prep time: 10 minutes

Cooking time: 5 minutes

Servings: 8

Nutrition facts per serving:

Total Carbs – 2 g

Net Carbs – 1.7 g

Fat – 7.3 g

Protein – 9.4 g

Calories –106

Ingredients:

- 2 cans (6.7 oz) smoked sardines
- 1 cup cottage cheese
- 7 oz Greek yogurt
- 2 Tbsp lemon juice
- 8 Lettuce leaves, washed and dried

Instructions:

1. Add the sardines to a food processor. Add in cottage cheese, Greek yogurt and lemon juice.
2. Blend until smooth.
3. Transfer to a bowl and keep refrigerated.
4. Serve on lettuce leaves.

Bacon and Pâté Fat Bombs

Prep time: 20 minutes (+ 30 minutes)

Cooking time: 35 minutes

Servings: 6

Nutrients per serving:

Total Carbs –.,4 g

Net Carbs – 1.2 g

Fat – 19.8 g

Protein – 7 g

Calories – 213

Ingredients:

- 4 large bacon slices
- ⅓ cup unsalted butter, divided
- 5½ oz chicken livers, diced
- ½ onion, diced
- 2 garlic cloves, chopped
- 1 tbsp fresh sage, chopped
- Salt, pepper to taste

Instructions:

1. Preheat the oven to 325°F. Cook the bacon slices on a baking sheet for 30 minutes. Crumble the bacon. Reserve the bacon grease.
2. In a skillet, heat half of the butter. Add the livers. Cook for 5 minutes. Transfer to a blender and pulse.
3. In another skillet, combine the remaining butter, onion, and garlic. Cook for 10 minutes. Transfer to a blender, add the bacon grease and the remaining ingredients except for the bacon and pulse. Refrigerate for 30 minutes.
4. Make 6 fat bombs from the mixture. Roll them in the crumbled bacon. Serve or store in the fridge for up to 5 days.

Tuna & Olive Endive Cups

Prep time: 5 minutes

Cooking time: none

Servings: 4

Nutrients per serving:

Total Carbs – 1 g

Net Carbs –0.8 g

Fat – 2 g

Protein – 2 g

Calories – 29

Ingredients:

- 1 oz canned tuna in olive oil, drained
- 6 large kalamata olives, pitted
- ½ Tbsp chopped green onion
- 1 tsp extra-virgin olive oil
- 4 Belgian endive leaves, washed and dried

Instructions:

1. In a food processor, combine all ingredients.
2. Scoop 1 Tbsp tuna mix onto each endive leaf.
3. Serve.

Smoked Salmon Canapés

Prep time: 5 minutes

Cooking time: none

Servings: 4

Nutrients per serving:

Total Carbs – 5 g

Net Carbs – 3.6 g

Fat – 2.4 g

Protein – 2.6 g

Calories – 51

Ingredients:

- 6 oz smoked salmon, cut into small squares
- 1 avocado, halved, pitted
- 1 cucumber, sliced in rounds
- 10 black olives, chopped
- 1 tsp lemon juice
- 1 sprig fresh dill

Instructions:

1. Mash avocado with lemon juice.
2. Combine smoked salmon and olives with avocado.
3. Spread a thin layer of avocado salmon mixture on a cucumber slice.
4. Decorate with fresh dill.

Creamy Tuna Endive Cups

Prep time: 5 minutes

Cooking time: none

Servings: 4

Nutrients per serving:

Total Carbs – 2 g

Net Carbs –1 g

Fat – 3 g

Protein – 3 g

Calories – 46

Ingredients:

- 1 oz canned tuna in olive oil, drained
- 1 oz cream cheese
- 4 Belgian endive leaves, washed and dried
- 2 Tbsp hemp hearts

Instructions:

1. In a small food processor, mix tuna and cream cheese until well blended.
2. Scoop 1 Tbsp tuna cream onto each endive cup.
3. Sprinkle ½ Tbsp hemp hearts over each endive cup. Serve immediately.

Smoked Mackerel Pâté Fat Bombs

Prep time: 10 minutes (+ 30 minutes)

Cooking time: none

Servings: 6

Nutrients per serving:

Total Carbs – 0.8 g

Net Carbs – 0.7 g

Fat – 17.3 g

Protein – 4.9 g

Calories – 161

Ingredients:

- 3½ oz full-fat cream cheese
- ¼ cup unsalted butter
- 1 mackerel fillet, smoked
- 1 tbsp lime juice
- 2 tbsp fresh chives, chopped
- 6 cucumber slices

Instructions:

1. In a food processor, blend first four ingredients.
2. In a bowl, combine the mixture with the chives, and mix with a spoon. Refrigerate for 30 minutes.
3. Serve as a dip with cucumber slices or store in an airtight container in the fridge for up to a week.

Creamy & Crunchy Egg Balls

Prep time: 40 minutes

Cooking time: none

Servings: 6

Nutrients per serving:

Total Carbs – 0 g

Net Carbs – 0 g

Fat – 6 g

Protein – 4 g

Calories – 67

Ingredients:

- 2 medium hard-boiled eggs
- 2 Tbsp cream cheese
- 1 Tbsp coconut oil, melted
- 2 slices prosciutto, cooked, crumbled

Instructions:

1. Place eggs, cream cheese, and coconut oil in a food processor and pulse until well mixed.
2. Refrigerate mixture for 30 minutes, or until it solidifies.
3. Once the egg mixture is solid, remove from refrigerator and shape into 6 balls.
4. Place prosciutto crumbles on a medium plate and roll individual balls through to coat.
5. Serve immediately or refrigerate in an airtight container up to 4 days.

Kalamata Olive and Feta Balls

Prep time: 2 hours 5 minutes

Cooking time: none

Servings: 6

Nutrients per serving:

Total Carbs – 2 g

Net Carbs – 0 g

Fat – 5 g

Protein – 2 g

Calories – 61

Ingredients:

- 2 oz cream cheese
- 2 oz feta
- 12 large kalamata olives, pitted
- ⅛ tsp fresh thyme,finely chopped
- ⅛ tsp fresh lemon zest

Instructions:

1. In a food processor, combine all ingredients until a coarse, doughy mix is made, about 30 seconds.
2. Transfer the mixture to a small bowl, then refrigerate 2 hours.
3. Form into 6 balls.
4. Serve or refrigerate up to 3 days.

Olive Dynamite Prosciutto Cup

Prep time: 20 minutes

Cooking time: 12 minutes

Servings: 1

Nutrients per serving:

Total Carbs – 8 g

Net Carbs – 4 g

Fat – 16 g

Protein – 8 g

Calories – 209

Ingredients:

- 1 slice prosciutto
- 1 medium egg yolk
- 1 Tbsp olive oil mayonnaise
- 4 large kalamata olives, pitted and chopped
- ¼ tsp Herbes de Provence

Instructions:

1. Preheat oven to 350°F.
2. Fold prosciutto slice in half, so it becomes almost square.
3. Place it in a muffin tin hole to line it completely.
4. Place egg yolk into prosciutto cup.
5. Gently place mayonnaise and olives on top of the egg. Sprinkle with Herbes de Provence.
6. Bake about 12 minutes, until egg yolk is still runny but warm.
7. Set aside for 15 minutes before removing from muffin pan.

Zucchini Fat Bombs

Prep time: 5 minutes (+ 2 hours)

Cooking time: 30 minutes

Servings: 12

Nutrients per serving:

Total Carbs – 2.5 g

Net Carbs – 0.48 g

Fat – 13.65 g

Protein – 2 g

Calories – 157

Ingredients:

- 1 zucchini
- 3½ oz cream cheese
- 1 oz Cheddar cheese
- 1 oz Parmesan cheese
- 1½ oz unsalted butter
- Salt to taste

Instructions:

1. Slice zucchini. In a nonstick pan lay slices of zucchini in rows—each with a bit of butter on top and bottom.
2. Add cream cheese and Cheddar in the center of each slice, and then sprinkle Parmesan cheese all over. Season with salt.
3. Heat the oven to 220°F. Cook for 30 minutes or until golden. Let cool and serve.

Baked Brie and Pecan Prosciutto Cup

Prep time: 20 minutes

Cooking time: 12 minutes

Servings: 1

Nutrients per serving:

Total Carbs – 2 g

Net Carbs – 1 g

Fat – 15 g

Protein – 12 g

Calories – 182

Ingredients:

- 1 slice prosciutto
- 1 oz Brie, diced with white skin on
- 6 pecan halves
- ⅛ tsp freshly ground black pepper

Instructions:

1. Preheat oven to 350°F.
2. Fold prosciutto slice in half, so it becomes almost square.
3. Place it in muffin tin hole to line it completely.
4. Place Brie in the prosciutto-lined cup.
5. Stick pecan halves in amongst Brie.
6. Bake about 12 minutes, until Brie is melted and prosciutto is cooked.
7. Let cool 10 minutes before removing from muffin pan.

Cream Cheese Fat Bombs

Prep time: 15 minutes (+ 30 minutes)

Cooking time: none

Servings: 24

Nutrients per serving:

Total Carbs – 4 g

Net Carbs – 2.5 g

Fat – 19.3 g

Protein – 4.5 g

Calories – 193

Ingredients:

- 3 oz full-fat cream cheese
- 2 tbsp unsalted butter
- ½ cup blue cheese, crumbled
- ¼ tsp garlic powder
- ¼ tsp onion powder
- 2 tbsp chives, chopped
- ⅔ cup pecans, chopped
- Salt, pepper to taste

Instructions:

1. Mash together the cream cheese and butter.
2. Add the remaining ingredients except for pecans. Mix well. Refrigerate 30 minutes.
3. Make 6 balls out of the mixture. Roll the balls in the chopped pecans. Serve.

Cheesy Muffin Prosciutto Cup

Prep time: 20 minutes

Cooking time: 12 minutes

Servings: 1

Nutrients per serving:

Total Carbs – 2 g

Net Carbs – 1 g

Fat – 15 g

Protein – 18 g

Calories – 218

Ingredients:

- 1 slice prosciutto
- 1 medium egg yolk
- ½ oz diced Brie
- ⅓ oz diced mozzarella
- ½ oz grated Parmesan

Instructions:

1. Preheat oven to 350°F.
2. Fold prosciutto slice in half, so it becomes almost square.
3. Place it in muffin tin hole to line it completely.
4. Place egg yolk into prosciutto cup.
5. Add cheeses on top of egg yolk without breaking it.
6. Bake about 12 minutes, until yolk is cooked and warm but still runny.
7. Set aside for 15 minutes before removing from muffin pan.

Jalapeño Pepper Fat Bombs

Prep time: 20 minutes

Cooking time: 5 minutes

Servings: 6

Nutrients per serving:

Total Carbs – 2.36 g

Net Carbs – 2.13 g

Fat – 13.3 g

Protein – 4.77 g

Calories – 147

Ingredients:

- 3 oz cream cheese
- 3 slices bacon
- 1 jalapeño pepper, seeded
- ½ tsp parsley, dried
- ¼ tsp onion powder
- ¼ tsp garlic powder
- Salt, pepper to taste

Instructions:

1. Fry bacon slices for 5 minutes, then place them on paper towels. Save bacon grease.
2. Chop the jalapeño pepper. Mix together with cream cheese, bacon fat, and spices.
3. Make balls out of cream cheese mixture and roll them in the crumbled bacon. Serve or store refrigerated in a container.

Quattro Formaggi Rollups

Prep time: 5 minutes

Cooking time: 5 minutes

Servings: 2

Nutrients per serving:

Total Carbs –1 g

Net Carbs –1 g

Fat – 13 g

Protein – 9 g

Calories – 152

Ingredients:

- 1 large egg
- 1 Tbsp Parmesan, grated
- 1 Tbsp blue cheese, crumbled
- 1 tsp butter
- 1 Tbsp mascarpone
- 1 oz Brie, thinly sliced

Instructions:

1. In a small bowl, whisk egg, Parmesan, and blue cheese until foamy.
2. Heat a small nonstick skillet over high heat and melt butter.
3. Pour in egg mixture, spreading evenly, so it forms a thin, even layer.
4. Once the first side is cooked, about 1 minute, flip frittata.
5. Spread mascarpone on top of the frittata, then place Brie slices in the middle and cover with a lid.
6. Cook until golden on bottom, about 2 more minutes.
7. Remove frittata to a plate.
8. Roll frittata into a tight roll, cut into 2 pieces and serve immediately while hot.

Broiled Bacon Wraps with Dates

Prep time: 40 minutes

Cooking time: 15 minutes

Servings: 6

Nutrition facts per serving:

Total Carbs – 5 g

Net Carbs – 4.5 g

Fat – 10 g

Protein – 19 g

Calories – 203

Ingredients:

- 8 oz dates, pitted, slit
- 1 lb bacon, sliced

Instructions:

1. Wrap each date with ½ slice bacon and secure with a toothpick.
2. Arrange the bacon wraps on a baking tray and bake at 425°F for 15-18 minutes.

Mascarpone Balls

Prep time: 20 minutes

Cooking time: none

Servings: 12

Nutrients per serving:

Total Carbs –2 g

Net Carbs –1 g

Fat –13

Protein – 2 g

Calories – 124

Ingredients:

- 6 Tbsp mascarpone
- 3 Tbsp sunflower seed butter
- 6 Tbsp coconut oil, softened
- 3 Tbsp unsweetened shredded coconut flakes

Instructions:

1. In a medium bowl, mix mascarpone, sunflower seed butter, and coconut oil until smooth paste forms.
2. Shape paste into 12 walnut-sized balls.
3. Spread coconut flakes on a medium plate and roll individual balls through to coat evenly.

Mediterranean Fat Bombs

Prep time: 10 minutes (+30 minutes)

Cooking time: none

Servings: 5

Nutrients per serving:

Total Carbs – 2 g

Net Carbs – 1.7 g

Fat – 17.1 g

Protein – 3.7 g

Calories – 164

Ingredients:

- ½ cup full-fat cream cheese
- ¼ cup butter
- 2 tsp dried herbs
- 4 sun-dried tomatoes, chopped
- 4 kalamata olives, chopped
- 2 cloves garlic, crushed
- 5 tbsp Parmesan cheese, grated
- Salt, pepper to taste

Instructions:

1. Combine butter with the cream cheese. Mash with a fork to mix.
2. Mix in remaining ingredients except for the Parmesan cheese. Refrigerate 30 minutes.
3. Create 5 balls out of the cheese mixture. Cover each ball with the grated parmesan cheese.
4. Serve or store in a container in the refrigerator

Salami & Olive Rollups

Prep time: 5 minutes

Cooking time: none

Servings: 3

Nutrients per serving:

Total Carbs – 6 g

Net Carbs – 2.4 g

Fat – 20 g

Protein – 8 g

Calories – 233

Ingredients:

- 12 large kalamata olives, pitted
- 3 oz cream cheese
- 3 (1-oz) slices Italian salami

Instructions:

1. In a small food processor, mix olives and cream cheese until they form a coarse mixture, about 10 seconds.
2. Form cheese mixture into 3 balls.
3. Place each ball on a slice of salami, then roll salami around it and secure with a toothpick.
4. Serve or refrigerate up to 3 days.

Bacon & Guacamole Fat Bombs

Prep time: 10 minutes (+ 30 minutes)

Cooking time: 15 minutes

Servings: 6

Nutrients per serving:

Total Carbs – 2.7 g

Net Carbs – 1.4 g

Fat – 15.2 g

Protein – 3.4 g

Calories – 156

Ingredients:

- ½ avocado, peeled, halved
- ¼ cup butter
- 2 cloves garlic, crushed
- 1 chili pepper, chopped
- 2 tbsp cilantro, chopped
- 1 tbsp lime juice
- ½ onion, diced
- 4 slices bacon
- Salt, pepper to taste

Instructions:

1. Preheat the oven to 375°F.
2. Cook the bacon strips on a baking tray for 15 minutes. Reserve the grease.
3. Combine the first six ingredients. Season with salt, pepper to taste and mix.
4. Add the onion and the bacon grease and mix. Refrigerate for 20-30 minutes.
5. Crumble the bacon. Create 6 balls from the mixture. Roll each ball in the bacon crumbles.
6. Serve.

Smoked Salmon & Avocado Rollups

Prep time: 5 minutes

Cooking time: none

Servings: 3

Nutrients per serving:

Total Carbs – 2 g

Net Carbs – 0 g

Fat – 5 g

Protein – 6 g

Calories – 78

Ingredients:

- 3 oz avocado flesh
- 1 tsp fresh lemon juice
- ⅛ tsp sea salt
- 3 slices smoked salmon (lox), about 1 oz each

Instructions:

1. In a bowl, combine avocado, lemon juice, and salt.
2. Spread avocado mixture evenly on top of each salmon slice.
3. Roll slices into individual rolls and secure with a toothpick.
4. Serve immediately.

Bacon & Egg Fat Bombs

Prep time: 10 minutes (+ 30 minutes)

Cooking time: 15 minutes

Servings: 6

Nutrients per serving:

Total Carbs – 0.2 g

Net Carbs – 0.2 g

Fat – 18.4 g

Protein – 5 g

Calories – 185

Ingredients:

- 2 large eggs, hard-boiled, cut into quarters
- ¼ cup butter
- 2 tbsp mayonnaise
- 4 large slices bacon
- Salt, pepper to taste

Instructions:

1. Preheat the oven to 375 °F.
2. Cook the bacon strips on a baking tray for 15 minutes. Reserve the grease.
3. Cut the butter into pieces and add the quartered eggs. Mash with a fork to mix.
4. Add the remaining ingredients except for the bacon and mix. Pour in the bacon grease. Mix well. Refrigerate for 20-30 minutes.
5. Crumble the bacon. Create 6 balls from egg mixture and roll each ball in the bacon crumbles.
6. Serve.

Mediterranean Rollups

Prep time: 7 minutes

Cooking time: 3 minutes

Servings: 2

Nutrients per serving:

Total Carbs – 14 g

Net Carbs – 4 g

Fat – 10 g

Protein –5 g

Calories – 153

Ingredients:

- 1 large egg
- 1 Tbsp extra-virgin olive oil
- ⅛ tsp sea salt
- 6 large kalamata olives, pitted
- 1 oz sun-dried tomatoes in oil
- ⅛ tsp red chili flakes
- ⅛ tsp parsley flakes

Instructions:

1. In a small bowl, combine egg, olive oil, and salt, and whisk until foamy.
2. Heat a small nonstick skillet over high heat and pour in egg mixture, spreading evenly, so it forms a thin, even layer.
3. Once the first side is cooked, about 1 minute, flip frittata and cook until golden on bottom, about 2 more minutes.
4. Remove frittata to a plate.
5. In a small food processor, mix olives, tomatoes, chili flakes, and parsley. Blend until well chopped and blended, about 30 seconds.
6. Spread olive paste on top of frittata in an even layer.
7. Roll frittata into a tight roll, cut into 2 pieces and serve immediately.

CONCLUSION

Thank you for reading this book and having the patience to try the recipes.

I do hope that you gain as much enjoyment reading and experimenting with the meals as I have had writing this book.

If you would like to leave a comment, you can do it at the Order section->Digital orders, in your amazon account.

Stay safe and healthy!

Recipe Index

Conversion Tables

VOLUME EQUIVALENTS (LIQUID)

US STANDARD	US STANDARD (OUNCES)	METRIC
2 tablespoons	1 fl. oz.	30 mL
¼ cup	2 fl. oz.	60 mL
½ cup	4 fl. oz.	120 mL
1 cup	8 fl. oz.	240mL
1½ cups	12 fl. oz.	355 mL
2 cups or 1 pint	16 fl. oz.	475 mL
4 cups or 1 quart	32 fl. oz.	1 L
1 gallon	128 fl. oz.	4 L

OVEN TEMPERATURES

FAHRENHEIT (°F)	CELSIUS (°C) APPROXIMATE
250 °F	120 °C
300 °F	150 °C
325 °F	165 °C
350 °F	180 °C
375 °F	190 °C
400 °F	200 °C
425 °F	220 °C
450 °F	230 °C

VOLUME EQUIVALENTS (LIQUID)

US STANDARD	METRIC (APPROXIMATE)
1/8 teaspoon	0.5 mL
¼ teaspoon	1 mL
½ teaspoon	2 mL
2/3 teaspoon	4 mL
1 teaspoon	5 mL
1 tablespoon	15 mL
¼ cup	59 mL
1/3 cup	79 mL
½ cup	118 mL
2/3 cup	156 mL
¾ cup	177 mL
1 cup	235 mL
2 cups or 1 pint	475 mL
3 cups	700 mL
4 cups or 1 quart	1 L
½ gallon	2 L
1 gallon	4 L

WEIGHT EQUIVALENTS

US STANDARD	METRIC (APPROXIMATE)
½ ounce	15 g
1 ounce	30 g
2 ounces	60 g
4 ounces	115 g
8 ounces	225 g
12 ounces	340 g
16 ounces or 1 pound	455 g

Other Books by Kaitlyn Donnelly

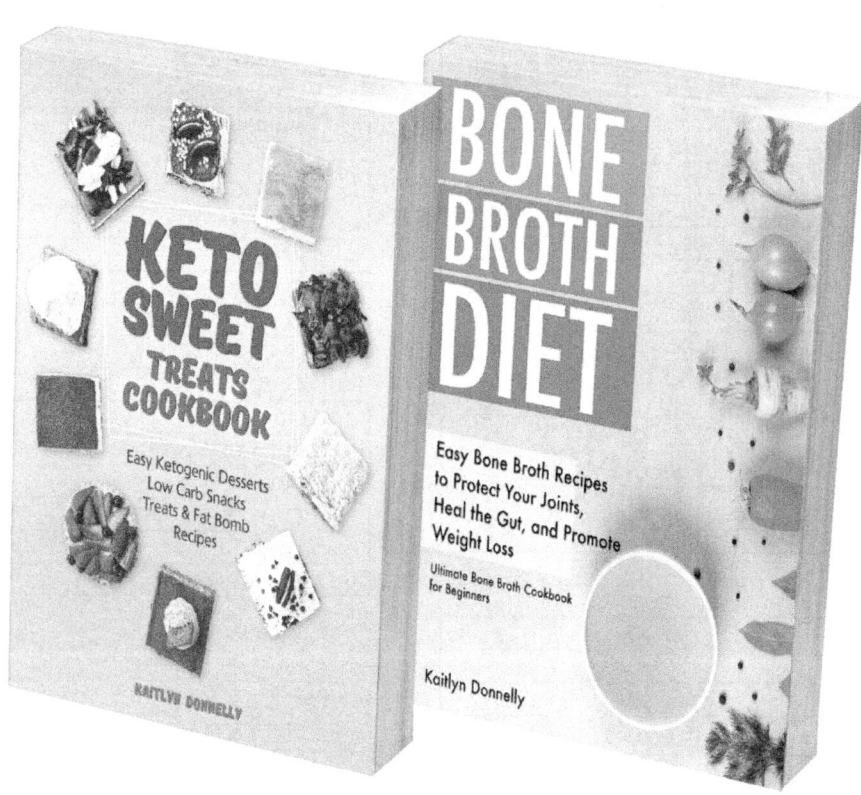

Made in the USA
Las Vegas, NV
10 January 2021